The End Is Not Yet

(Fall 2015 Edition)

Also by the Author

Judgment Day? Not Yet:
Why the Rapture Won't Happen on May 21, 2011
(Smashwords, 2011)

The End Is Not Yet

(Fall 2015 Edition)

Why the Four Blood Moons and the Shemitah Year Do <u>Not</u> Mean that the Economy Will Collapse, World War III Will Break Out, the Antichrist Shall Arise, or the Messiah Will Come

Mark E. Koltko-Rivera, Ph.D.

Exploration Media
an imprint of
LVX MEDIA
2015

The End Is Not Yet (Fall 2015 Edition):
Why the Four Blood Moons and the Shemitah Year Do <u>Not</u> Mean that the Economy Will Collapse, World War III Will Break Out, the Antichrist Shall Arise, or the Messiah Will Come.
by Mark E. Koltko-Rivera, Ph.D.
First edition, published September 2015 by Exploration Media, an imprint of LVX Media.

ISBN-13: 978-0-6925-3772-5
ISBN-10: 0-6925-3772-4
U.S. editions printed in the United States of America.

Back cover author photo by Katherine Finkelstein:
    katherinefinkelstein.com

www.KoltkoRivera.com

Copies of this book may be purchased online at:
    http://astore.amazon.com/marswri-20

Booksellers: Check with your distributor for this book.

Dedicated

to everyone who really studies both
Science and the Bible

and to the memory of
Richard Luman
late chair of the
Department of Religion
Haverford College
Requiescat in Pacem, Magister et Amice

Table of Contents

Preface

In this book, I take on claims that the latter half of September 2015 will see a collection of cataclysms: another catastrophic financial meltdown; war involving; the rise of the Antichrist; the Coming of the Messiah; a major climate disaster; even killer comets and asteroids, prodded to crash into the Earth by a rogue planet or star. Anecdotal accounts inform me that many people are being misled by such claims; reportedly, some people have caught the hysterical spirit in which some Internet commentators have made these predictions, and have acted accordingly (for example, selling all their possessions and building underground bunkers).

In the past, over the course of several such predictions of the End, hysteria has led some people to take rash, ill-considered actions that could not be undone (some of which I describe below). Part of why I wrote this book is to forestall such behavior as the supposed critical dates approach.

This is not the first time I have done this sort of thing. When the late Harold Camping predicted that Judgment Day would come on May 21, 2011, I wrote the book *Judgment Day? Not Yet*,[1] explaining how Mr. Camping had seriously misinterpreted the Bible and its symbolism. Because the current claims about the Fall of 2015 are so much more detailed, and cover a much wider range of phenomena, than Camping's

---

[1]   Koltko-Rivera (2011). Some of this Preface is taken from the Introduction to that book.

claims, in this book I consider not only biblical interpretation, but also various aspects of history and human psychology.

But why should I care? Why not just leave the believers in these dire predictions in their mistaken beliefs? After all, when all the disasters fail to occur on schedule, no harm will be done, right?

Wrong.

There are several ways in which false predictions like these might cause harm:

1. **People who expect imminent disaster sometimes take lethal actions.** For example, in 1994 and 1997, members of the Order of the Solar Temple committed mass murder and mass suicide involving both adult members and their children, apparently believing that the world was soon to face a catastrophic environmental disaster. It is often overlooked that the Solar Temple considered itself to be a Christian group, which had as one of its purposes preparation for the Second Coming of Jesus Christ.[2] It is well-known that the Aum Shinrikyo group (now known as Aleph) in Japan carried out attacks with deadly sarin gas on the Tokyo subway in 1995. However, it is not as widely known that these attacks occurred two years before a global nuclear Armageddon was predicted to happen, according to the group's leader.[3]

2. **People who expect the end of the world sometimes take other drastic and ill-considered actions.** For example, in 1988, the late Edgar C. Whisenant, a former NASA engineer, predicted that the Rapture would occur during the Jew-

---

[2]   "Order of the Solar Temple" (2011).
[3]   "Aum Shinrikyo" (2011).

ish New Year in mid-September of 1988.[4] In Florida at the time, it was reported that some people who believed this prediction amassed huge credit card debts, expecting that they would have no need to repay once the Rapture had occurred. One can only imagine their surprise (and the size of their credit card statements) when the predicted Rapture did not happen. Although it can be argued that these individuals only brought their subsequent misery upon themselves, we should also consider the collateral damage inflicted upon their innocent family members, as all these parties were burdened with the fallout of the subsequent bankruptcies. In 2011, one of Mr. Camping's radio listeners in New York City sunk his life savings, amounting to at least $140,000, into subway, bus, and bus shelter advertisements which proclaimed May 21 as the Judgment Day.[5] One can only hope that this then-60-year-old gentleman had a backup retirement plan.

3. **Focus on false predictions distracts us from the very real problems that our world faces.** This point was brought home during the Camping incident when a *Washington Post* reader complained that Family Radio's Project Caravan (in which buses covered in Camping's message cruised the streets of major cities) received much more press coverage, while local efforts to counteract global warming were largely ignored. [6] Our world truly does face major crises involving the natural environment, economics, politics, and matters of war versus peace. With only limited capacities for attention, we need to focus on real issues, not fake ones.

---

4   "Edgar C. Whisenant" (2015).
5   Campbell & Sanderson, 2011; Graves & Alpert, 2011.
6   Heald, 2011.

These three ways that false predictions of doom cause harm would be problems from anyone's point of view, regardless of their religious beliefs or lack thereof. No reasonable person wants to see others commit murder or suicide based on mistaken perceptions of the future, or burden themselves and others with huge, unnecessary debt. I would think that everyone would want people to focus on addressing the real problems and challenges that we face in the world, rather than fantasy problems.

However, from a Christian point of view, there are two other ways in which false predictions of doom cause harm:

4. **False predictions of Judgment Day, the Rapture, or the end of the world bring ridicule upon the reputations of the Bible, its believers, and real biblical prophecies.** Every time someone falsely predicts catastrophes on the supposed basis of some aspect of the Bible, people come to ridicule, not just the false prediction, but the Bible itself. As the Rev. Lynn Eynon, pastor of Woodstock Christian Church, said during the Camping incident, "It makes Christianity look silly."[7] Back in 2011, for example, the American Atheists organization held parties in several states on the theme, "Another Rapture That Wasn't."[8] On Facebook at that time, groups formed around such themes as "Pre-Rapture Orgy"[9]; I myself received a Facebook invitation to a "Post-Rapture Looting," which over 17,000 people "Liked" as of early May 21, 2011.[10]

---

[7]   Quoted in Poole, 2011, par. 11.

[8]   Poole, 2011, par. 16.

[9]   Goffard, 2011, par. 17.

[10]   As of September 10, 2015, this Facebook "Community" was still in existence at https://www.facebook.com/Post-Rapture-Looting-116030068480558/ , and had 18,015 "Likes."

Each such occasion desensitizes people to the importance of Biblical prophecy, which is itself a serious problem from a Christian point of view. In addition, each false prediction of the Rapture or Judgment Day makes it that much more difficult to spread the Christian message with credibility. Speaking as a former missionary myself, having preached Christianity for years in East Asia, I know that it can be challenging enough to share the Gospel under the best of circumstances; it is all the more difficult when some ill-conceived prediction of doom brings ridicule upon Christianity.

5. **To focus on false predictions diverts attention from the real Christian message.** It is a stunted form of Christianity that tries to bring people to repentance through fear of the Judgment Day. The New Testament consistently teaches that Christians are to preach a message of hope, not apocalyptic terror. Yes, there are prophecies of very hard times ahead. However, these prophecies are given to comfort the believers and help them to prepare, without fear. Christianity is about the Good News concerning Jesus Christ, our Exemplar and Savior. We lose focus on these things when we put too much emphasis on fear of a supposedly impending Judgment Day and the end of the world. It may have been to prevent this kind of lopsided emphasis that the Jesus taught that we would not know the day or hour of his Second Coming.[11]

Given all these issues, I thought it worthwhile to prepare this guide to the claims being made about the catastrophes that have been predicted for September 2015.

Who am I to take on this task? As it happens, I have qualifications in several areas relevant to these issues. In my undergraduate years, I studied biblical Hebrew and New Testa-

---

[11]   In the Bible: Matthew 24: 36, 42; Acts 1:6-7.

ment Greek. Having served as a missionary in East Asia, I am familiar with the Christian scriptures. My graduate training is in psychology, and this has made me familiar with the common mental mechanisms that set people up to believe things that have little if any grounding in reality. Finally, my work as a psychological researcher has given me a strong background in scientific logic and reasoning.

In terms of my background and approach: I am a practicing Christian, specifically a Latter-day Saint. At the same time, I write this book not just for Christians, but for everyone. I do not see this book as the proper place to present, explain, or defend the Christian message, but rather as a place to deal with some highly problematic ideas in a way that everyone can find useful. There are a few, clearly labeled places where I speak specifically to the Christian community.

I do not expect anyone to accept what I say, based on my word. I invite readers to look at these issues with open minds.

Unless otherwise noted, all biblical quotations in English are from the King James Version (KJV), also known as the Authorised Version (AV), first printed in 1611.

Of course, I bear sole responsibility for any errors of fact or interpretation in this book.

—Mark E. Koltko-Rivera, Ph.D.
September 18, 2015
www.KoltkoRivera.com

The End Is Not Yet

(Fall 2015 Edition)

Introduction

Over the last two years or so, with increasing frequency (and, it must be said, hysteria), large numbers of people have proclaimed on radio and video that there are an unusual number of significant events occurring in the last half of September, 2015—and that these events, especially as a group, signal forthcoming disaster. For some, these catastrophes involve American domestic politics and international relations; for others, they involve the national and global economy; some believe that these events foreshadow the rise of the long-prophesied Antichrist, or the coming of the Messiah; for still others, these events are portents of widespread destruction, perhaps even the end of the Earth itself, and all life thereon.

In this book, I say the following about these ideas:

1. To a large extent, these claims are based on a misunderstanding of (a) the Bible, (b) the calendar and other traditions of the Jewish people, and/or (c) the facts of history.

2. There are important reasons why people fall for ideas like this, reasons that involve (a) a general lack of understanding of the Bible, (b) a generally poor understanding of history, and/or (c) some quirks in the way that the human mind works.

3. There are indeed serious risks to the well-being of the human race in our day—but there are

positive and productive ways for ordinary people and their elected representatives to deal with them.

4. The   claims that the doomsayers make are simply not true. The global economy will not collapse, global war will not occur, the Antichrist will not come to power, the Messiah will not suddenly arrive, and the world will not end—at least, not during the Fall of 2015.

One of the marks of a mature mind is that it does not take any extraordinary claim to be true, just based on someone's say-so. One of the problems in our society is that many people simply accept the claims of supposed experts without a critical investigation of their claims and assumptions.

I do not expect anyone to take *my* word for any of the claims that I make, either. I have laid out all my sources for any reader to check. Indeed, my greatest recommendation is for you, the reader, to learn about the issues, take no one's word for anything (from science to history to biblical interpretation), apply reason and logic and the rules of evidence to what you have heard, check sources and assumptions, and come to your own conclusions, rather than just believing what anyone tells you (including myself).

1

Economic Meltdown: The Shemitah Cycle

One of the most frequently made claims about Fall 2015 is that this period will see the beginnings of economic catastrophe, as supposedly predicted by the finer points of the traditional Jewish calendar system (particularly the conclusion of the recurring seven-year cycle that ends in the Shemitah year), and by the co-occurrence of certain events with these calendar dates. In this chapter, I investigate these claims; describe what is true and what is not; explain what is at stake when people give credence to the false Shemitah economic disaster hypothesis; explain why so many people believe such claims anyway; and suggest what the reader might do to address the danger of economic instability in a positive and productive way.

The Claims

It has been claimed that there is a seven-year economic cycle laid out in the Bible, and that the end of the seventh year in this cycle portends a time of economic upheaval. This is what I call **the Shemitah economic disaster hypothesis**, or simply **the Shemitah theory**. The people who believe this hypothesis base their claims on the biblical laws pertaining to the sabbatical year dictated in the Bible, known as the Shemitah year (pronounced "shmee-TAH," spelled variously). They claim that the end of the current Shemitah year—which did indeed occur on Sunday, September 13, 2015—will be followed by economic catastrophe.

As evidence for these claims, some point out that at the end of the most recent preceding two Shemitah years—in September of 2001, and September of 2008—there were cataclysmic economic disruptions. Some claim that there is a pattern of economic upheaval, particularly in the United States, coinciding with the conclusion of the Shemitah year, going back for generations.[12] It has been claimed that a statistician, Thomas Pound, proved statistically "that the sabbatical years were the only group of years in which the market cycle averages consistent significant losses since 1871."[13]

What Is True About the Shemitah Claims

Some aspects of these claims are actually true. Other aspects are completely false. Let us pull the strands of this claim apart and investigate them bit by bit.

The Shemitah Year is a Real Thing— in Biblical Laws About Agriculture

There really is such a thing as the Shemitah year defined in the Bible, and the religious laws pertaining to it are observed by many people to this day in the modern state of Israel. In the Jewish calendar, the Shemitah year is the sabbatical year, the last year of a seven-year agricultural cycle defined in

---

[12]   Cahn (2014).

[13]   Hohmann (2015a), quoting Berkowitz (2015).

the Bible, which describes the Lord as giving Moses this law for Hebrews to observe in the Promised Land:

> And six years thou shalt sow thy land, and shalt gather in the fruits thereof:
>
> But the seventh year thou shalt let it rest and lie still; that the poor of thy people may eat: and what they leave the beasts of the field shall eat. In like manner thou shalt deal with thy vineyard, and with thy oliveyard.[14]

The Bible records a divine promise that, if the Hebrews observed the sabbatical year in the Promised Land, there would be enough food harvested during the sixth year of the cycle to last three full years.[15] During the sabbatical year, debts to other Israelites were also to be remitted,[16] and Hebrew slaves were to be freed.[17] In most years, the traditional Jewish year concludes, and a new year then begins, sometime during the month of September as defined in the Gregorian calendar (which is used by secular states in the West and elsewhere). The first Shemitah year that was observed in the modern state of Israel concluded in September 1952, at the end of the year 5712 of the Jewish calendar; every seven years thereafter has seen the conclusion of a Shemitah year, including September 2001, September 2008, and September 2015.[18]

---

14   In the Bible: Exodus 23:10-11.
15   In the Bible: Leviticus 25:20-22.
16   In the Bible: Deuteronomy 15:1-6.
17   In the Bible: Jeremiah 34:13-14.
18   "Shmita" (2015).

The Conclusion of Some Shemitah Years Actually Have Been Followed by Economic Upheavals

There certainly have been economic upheavals at the end of some Shemitah years. The Jewish year 5761 was a Shemitah year; the last day of that year—the 29th day of the month Elul—fell on September 17, 2001 of the secular calendar. On this very day, the Dow Jones Industrial Average, which had seen massive fall-offs following the September 11 attacks that year, showed the third largest daily point loss in its entire history, a record still held as I write these words in early September of 2015.[19] The airline and recreation/hospitality industries had suffered a sharp drop in business after terrorists used commercial jet airplanes as bombs in the Attack on America. The sharp decline in these industries' stocks dragged a good piece of the American economy down with them.[20]

The end of the Shemitah year of 5768 saw another major economic catastrophe. The 29th day of Elul, 5768, fell on September 29, 2008, in the Western calendar. This was the day in which the Dow Jones experienced what remains as the single largest daily point loss in its entire history,[21] during the free fall of the American stock markets that signaled the acute

---

[19] "Stock Market Crash History" (2014).

[20] These business declines had very real, personal consequences for millions of Americans. One of my own students at the University of Central Florida at that time had to withdraw from college to help with the family business—which supplied snacks to Disneyworld in Orlando. Disneyworld, of course was seeing a severe drop off in business at the time, because so many people refused to fly anywhere, even for vacation. No travelers, no one eating pretzels, no need for snacks.

[21] Clarke (2014).

phase of the global financial crisis of 2007-2008, the effects of which are very much still with us today as I write this.

There Are Certainly Problems with the Current Global and American Economies—and Things Could Indeed Get Worse

The current global and American economies certainly are in unsettled and vulnerable conditions. On the global stage during the summer of 2015, the showdown over the sovereign debt of the government of Greece, and the abrupt declines in the prices on the Chinese stock market, rattled nerves around the world. The American recovery from the global economic crisis of 2007 and thereafter continues to be lackluster. There are serious concerns that the technology sector is heavily overvalued, and thus is experiencing a bubble—and all bubbles pop, vanishing along with billions of dollars in value.[22]

But does any of this have anything to do with the Shemitah? As I show below—no, not really.

What Is False About the Shemitah Theory

There are several ways in which the Shemitah economic disaster hypothesis fails. First of all, let us consider the historical record: over the last century or so, have the end of Shemitah years been followed by economic distress? As we shall see, the end of a Shemitah year is a very poor indicator of impending economic doom.

---

[22]   Bilton (2015).

Some of the Very Worst Economic Catastrophes Have Not Been at the End of Shemitah Years

Some of the worst economic catastrophes in the Western world have not been associated with the end of Shemitah years at all. This calls into question the whole idea of the Shemitah year as a harbinger of economic trouble.

The Panic of 1873, which triggered a severe depression in Europe and North America that lasted for six and more years—an event so catastrophic that it was called "the Great Depression" until the events of the late 1920s and 1930s—occurred during the fifth year of a seven-year biblical cycle, nowhere near the end of a Shemitah year.[23]

The Panic of 1890 (also known as the Baring crisis) caused an acute recession in England and a worse depression in Argentina, with severe effects in Brazil. However, this occurred after the Barings Bank in London approached bankruptcy in November of 1890, two months into the second year of the seven-year biblical cycle—not a Shemitah year at all.

The Panic of 1893 was even worse than the Panic of 1873 for the United States, and constituted the most severe economic depression that the country had experienced up to that time. However, it occurred during the fourth year of a seven-year biblical cycle, as far away from the end of a Shemitah year as it is possible to be.

Of course, the worst economic crisis in the modern Western world was precipitated by the stock market crash beginning on October 24, 1929 ("Black Tuesday"), leading to the Great Depression that held the Western world in a death grip

---

[23]   I describe how I determine Shemitah years in the Appendix.

for a decade. However, Black Tuesday occurred about a month into the sixth year of the seven-year biblical cycle, nearly two years *before* the end of a Shemitah year.[24]

If the Shemitah is some kind of divine harbinger of economic distress—an idea promoted most prominently by Jonathan Cahn, author of the major book on this subject, *The Mystery of the Shemitah*—then how could this system of prophetic signs miss such widespread economic disasters as the Panics of 1873, 1890, and 1893, as well as the global *Great Depression?* That is four major economic disasters over a period of less than 60 years, and the Shemitah economic prediction system failed in every case.

If I had a house alarm system that failed in the face of four major burglaries over the course of my lifetime, I would discard the alarm system. (Frankly, I would replace it after the first failure.) People should do the same with the Shemitah economic disaster hypothesis on this basis alone.

In all fairness, it should be noted that Mr. Cahn seems to have anticipated this criticism. As he put it:

> … we cannot expect prophetic happenings to show up on a regular schedule or to perform on cue. Nothing significant has to happen within the Shemitah of 2014–2015. The phenomenon may manifest in one cycle, and not in another, and then again in the next. And the focus of the message is not date-setting but the call of God to repentance and return. At the same time, some-

---

[24] Mr. Cahn (2014, p. 83) tries to connect the Great Depression to the end of the Shemitah year which occurred on September 6, 1937—almost eight years after Black Tuesday. I consider this a stretch.

thing of significance could take place, and it is wise to note the times.[25]

I am all for repentance and return to God. However, this does seem a rather disingenuous comment for Mr. Cahn to make. At the point that he made this statement in *The Mystery of the Shemitah,* he had already spent about 240 pages explaining how the Shemitah cycle was supposedly behind every major market downturn of the last century of American history. To say at this point that "we cannot expect prophetic happenings to show up on a regular schedule" is to negate his entire argument.

But wait! There's more.

Some Shemitah Years Actually See *Improvements* in the Stock Market

Thomas Pound performed a statistical analysis of the years in the Shemitah cycle using a database of stock market data made available by Robert Shiller, Ph.D., the Nobel Prize-winning Sterling Professor of Economics at Yale University.[26] Shiller's database includes the Standard & Poor's Composite index for stocks, with monthly data from 1871 to the present.[27]

Analyzing Shiller's S&P Composite data myself, I made a fascinating finding. Yes, it was true that, over this period,

---

[25] Cahn (2014) p. 240.

[26] "Biographical Sketch" (n.d.).

[27] The database is available at http://www.econ.yale.edu/~shiller/data.htm ; select "U.S. Stock Markets 1871-Present and CAPE Ratio." The Excel spreadsheet for the database comes up as a graph; the viewer may then select the Data tab at the bottom left corner of the page to see specific figures for each year.

years which saw the conclusion of a Shemitah were the only years that, as a group, showed an average loss for the market. However, that was not the whole story by any means.

I found that, in the 20 instances in which Shemitah years occurred during the period 1871-2014, fully 7 of these cases (35%) showed a *gain* in the value of the S&P, compared to the value the previous year.[28] For years which showed a gain, the median gain was 15.2%, which is no mean feat.

This is hardly the unmitigated record of financial disaster that one would expect to follow the end of a Shemitah year, if one gave credence to those who believe in the Shemitah economic disaster hypothesis.

To Mr. Cahn and his followers, the end of a Shemitah year functions as a divine sign, a sort of alarm system that indicates coming economic problems. If I had an alarm system on my house, and if 35% of the time it issued a warning that turned out to be a false alarm, I would certainly replace it. People need to replace the Shemitah system with something else to tell them when economic problems are likely to occur.

That Statistician's Findings About Shemitah Years and the Economy Is Deeply Flawed

As I mentioned briefly above, the financial advisor Thomas Pound has been widely quoted in relation to research about the economic outcomes of Shemitah years. In an online report on his investment website, Pound reports that he compared three market cycle theories, including the Shemitah cycle, us-

---

[28]   These were the calendar years 1889, 1924, 1938, 1945, 1952, 1959, and 1980, during each of which a Shemitah year concluded in the Fall season. For each of these years, the year-end value of the S&P Composite was higher than the year-end value the year before.

ing Shiller's stock market data, going back to the year 1871.[29] Pound found one of the market cycle theories to be outright useless, although he reported that the other two, including the Shemitah cycle theory, were supported by the data.

As he stated it, the Shemitah cycle theory claims that "every seven years [that is, following the end of a Shemitah year], there is the potential for a market calamity".[30] He reported that he performed a statistical analysis of variance (ANOVA) test comparing each year in the seven-year cycle going back to 1871, and found that

> the sabbatical years are the only group of years where the cycle … averages a loss (-2.40% ±21.52%) since 1871. It is also the most volatile year of the cycle. The question is, though, are these differences significant? These differences are … significant ($p < .001$) ….[31]

As Mr. Pound told a reporter:

> "Statistically, it appears that the calendar years in which the Sabbatical year ends are worse than the other six years, and that difference is significant based on the data I have," Pound told *Breaking Israel News*.[32]

This statement has been widely repeated in various online news reports.[33]

---

29 Pound (2015).
30 Pound (2015).
31 Pound (2015).
32 Berkowitz (2015).
33 For example, Hohmann (2015a).

So, how real is this finding? As it happens, not very.

It is easy for people to sound as if they know what they are doing when they say that they conducted such-and-such a statistical test. The problem is that it is extremely easy to conduct the *wrong* statistical test for the specific situation before us, and that is the mistake that Mr. Pound has made. This error has serious consequences for his conclusion.

Every statistical test makes some assumptions about the data being analyzed. The ANOVA is no exception. Mr. Pound is not perfectly clear on this point, but I take it from his description of his research that he performed what is technically termed a 1-way ANOVA for independent groups. One assumption of this test which must never be violated is the idea that each of the groups being compared must be independent from each other group.[34] For example, within any given 7-year cycle, the stock value at the end of Year 1 of the Shemitah cycle must have absolutely nothing at all to do with the stock value at the end of Year 2, and so on.

Does this assumption fit the situation here? Of course not! It is only common sense to think that the stock values in Year 2 will depend, to some extent, on what the values were in Year 1. Stock values do not vary completely at random. For this reason alone, the 1-way independent groups ANOVA is completely inappropriate here, and results from such an analysis are meaningless and likely misleading.

To see whether this inappropriate test would indeed lead to the results that Mr. Pound reported, I conducted a very similar analysis. In my case, I analyzed a simpler variable than did Mr. Pound: the change, from one year to the next, of the S&P Composite index. (Thus, I did not make adjustments for reinvested dividends, as Mr. Pound did.) Using a 1-way

---

[34]   B. H. Cohen (2008) p. 360.

ANOVA for independent groups, I obtained similar results to what Mr. Pound obtained. Of course, because this situation violates the assumption of independent observations, my results were as meaningless as Mr. Pound's.

I then conducted an analysis that *is* designed to allow for situations where there is some sort of underlying connection across the groups being compared: the 1-way *repeated measures* ANOVA. Basically, this test treats each 7-year cycle as an experimental "subject," like a college student, who is tested at 7 different times. When I conducted this analysis, I found no statistically significant differences among the seven years of the Shemitah cycle. (That is, the differences that did exist among the different years of the cycle stood a good chance of being the products of chance.)

I give a formal report of my statistical analysis in the Appendix. The hypothesis that Shemitah years are harbingers of economic distress is simply not supported by the data.

Another aspect of my analysis was interesting, as well. I found that the typical Shemitah year is followed by a rather mild decline in the financial markets. Using data for the years 1876 through 2008 (which encompassed 19 full Shemitah cycles), I found that the median change in the S&P Composite index after the end of a Shemitah year was -2.8%. That's it: a market drop of less than 3%. By contrast, after the 9-11 attacks in 2001, the year-end market drop was 14%, and the drop in 2002 was even worse (21%); after the global financial meltdown began in earnest in 2008, the market drop for the year was a heart-stopping 41%. But these were very atypical for Shemitah years generally.

So, the typical outcome of a Shemitah year is a market drop of less than 3%. This is not desirable, to be sure, but it is hardly the territory of catastrophe, either.

Perhaps the most powerful refutation of a claim is to show that the claim is false, *even under the same assumptions that the claim uses*. The Shemitah theory's most important assumption is that the Bible is the word of God. Even on that basis, however, the Shemitah theory lacks support, as I show below.

There Is Nothing In the Bible to Support the Shemitah as a Prophetic Sign of American Economic Problems

The people who promote the Shemitah economic disaster hypothesis do so by unjustifiably reinterpreting both scripture and the facts of history. Jonathan Cahn's book *The Mystery of the Shemitah*, is an excellent example of both tendencies. Because these tendencies are central to his predictions about our economic future, I take the liberty of quoting him at length:

> In its first and original context the Shemitah is connected to Israel. It is the only nation commanded to observe it. … But we are not dealing here with the Shemitah as an observance but as a prophetic sign—particularly as a warning or manifestation of national judgment. Such a prophetic sign could be given to any nation as long as that nation in some way matched the description or shared the attributes of ancient Israel in 586 BC. In other words, it would have to be:
>
> • A nation warranting a prophetic warning or manifestation of judgment, a nation in defiance of God's ways

...

- A civilization established on the Word of God, dedicated to His purposes, and consecrated to His glory from its very inception

It can be argued that only two civilizations in human history were established, dedicated, and consecrated to the will, the word, the purposes, and the glory of God from the moment of their conceptions. The first was Israel; the second was America. American civilization was established and dedicated at Cape Henry, Plymouth, and Massachusetts Bay to the purposes of God. ... But let's take it even further:

- A civilization specifically established after the pattern of ancient Israel

Most would find it surprising to learn that America was consciously, intentionally, and specifically founded and formed after the pattern of ancient Israel. Its founders saw it as a new Israel, the Israel of the New World. It was their exodus from Europe like the Hebrew exodus from Egypt. The New World was their new promised land, and the Massachusetts Bay Colony was their New Jerusalem.[35]

Because so much is at stake here, I feel the need to refute Mr. Cahn's statement point by point.

---

[35] Cahn (2014) pp. 55-57.

There is absolutely no scriptural basis for the position that the Shemitah is a sign of future economic distress.

There is no way to say this nicely, so I shall state it bluntly: Everyone who claims that the end of a Shemitah year is some kind of divine harbinger of hard economic times is making this up out of thin air. *The Shemitah is not portrayed in the Bible as any kind of prophetic sign at all.*

Mr. Cahn offers not one shred of biblical evidence that the Shemitah is supposed to be taken as a "prophetic sign ... of national judgment." Sure, the Bible states that the ancient Israelites were given divine punishment because they did not *observe* the Shemitah law[36]—but this is a very far cry from making the end of the Shemitah year itself a *sign* that hard times would be coming!

Mr. Cahn claims that the meaning of the Shemitah came to him as a revelation which he recorded with over a dozen other revelations in his 2011 novel, *The Harbinger*.[37] Just because he claims to have a revelation does not mean that others ought to believe him. Is he claiming prophecy as a gift of the Spirit?[38] Then let him state that openly—and in the knowledge that, although anyone may claim to possess a gift of the Spirit, yet another such gift is the gift of "discerning of spirits," that is, the detection of such claims that are false.[39]

The Lord used Moses to reveal the Shemitah law to the ancient Hebrews. Is Mr. Cahn putting himself on the level of

---

[36]   In the Bible: Jeremiah 34:13-14; 2 Chronicles 36:19-21.

[37]   Cahn (2014) p. 3.

[38]   In Christian belief, prophecy is one of the gifts of the Holy Spirit; in the Bible: 1 Corinthians 12:8-10.

[39]   In the Bible: 1 Corinthians 12:10.

Moses, to reveal the supposed application of the Shemitah to the modern world?

The United States was not founded on the Word of God, nor was it modeled on ancient Israel.

It is certainly the custom in some circles to make the claim that "America is a Christian nation." *But this is not the case, nor has it ever <u>been</u> the case, except in a demographic sense.* There is much that could be said about this, but for the sake of space I shall mention only the following points:

- People of many different religions came to found the United States, entirely aside from the Puritans. Jews lived in European America from its earliest days. Catholics and Quakers—neither of whom the Puritans could tolerate—were here early on as well. Anglicans were here in large numbers as soon as British colonists arrived, with lesser numbers of Presbyterians. The Puritans were not the "founders" of America in any real sense.

- The United States was not founded on the Word of God. The Supreme Being is mentioned exactly four times in the Declaration of Independence—as "God," "Creator," "Supreme Judge of the World," and "divine Providence"—and each time the Supreme Being is named in general terms that would be applicable to believers in any religion at all. No mention is made of Jesus, Christianity, or the Bible.

- The foundational document of the United States is actually the Constitution, which establishes the form of our government and provides a framework of rights and responsibilities. No mention whatsoever is made in the Constitution about God, Jesus, Christianity, or the Bible. Beyond that, the Constitution specifically forbids Congress to make any law that privileges any religion over another, or that privileges believers in religion over nonbelievers. (That is precisely what the First Amendment is saying when it decrees that "Congress shall make no law respecting an establishment of religion": Congress cannot "establish" a religion, that is, make some religion special, more official, or favored in the eyes of the law.)

- The American founding fathers were not all the conventional Christians that popular myth would have us believe. Several of them found Deist and Unitarian thought appealing.[40] For anyone trying to make the case that America is a Christian nation, the founding fathers are a bad place to start.

In sum, Jonathan Cahn and his followers have no warrant for claiming some kind of mystical identity between the United States of America and the ancient people of Israel, a supposed identity that would somehow make the Shemitah laws relevant to the United States.

Statistical analysis—the voice of logic and reason—provides no evidence for the Shemitah economic disaster hypothesis. Scripture—the voice of faith—provides no evidence, either. The facts of history—the voice of experienced human reality—also fail to support this claim. In the face of this stun-

---

[40]   Holmes (2006).

ning lack of support for the Shemitah theory, the most sensible thing for people to do is to just ignore the Shemitah (unless they are farmers in the state of Israel), and focus instead on addressing real-life issues in an effective way.

Why This All Matters

The reader might well ask, why is it necessary to so thoroughly nail the coffin shut on the Shemitah theory? As it happens, there are very good reasons to do so.

We Should Take an Active Stance, Not a Passive One, to the World

One problem with ideas like the Shemitah theory is that it discourages people from action. If the end of a Shemitah year means economic disaster, then why bother trying to change things? The best thing you can do is accept the Lord's will, and try to minimize the damage for yourself and your family.

I am all for accepting the will of the Lord. But, as a Christian, I refuse to be passive about my life and the society I live in. Did not Jesus teach that his followers were to be "the salt of the earth," and "the light of the world"? Did he not command his followers to "let your light so shine before men"?[41]

Jesus taught his followers to be peacemakers.[42] Christians should take the lead to feed the hungry, clothe the naked (which is to say, care for the poor), take in the refugee ("I was a stranger, and ye took me in"), and tend to the prison popula-

---

[41] Jesus said these things in the Sermon on the Mount, as recorded in the Bible: See Matthew 5:13-16.

[42] In the Bible: Matthew 5:9.

tion and the sick.[43] The "true religion" of Christianity consists, in part, for caring for society's underdogs, exemplified for the Apostle James by the fatherless and widows.[44] In other words, Christians are not supposed to take the world and its evil, cruelty, and pain as a given.

For that matter, the people of *all* religions, as well as people who follow nontheistic ethics, are taught to increase the good in the world and reduce the bad. That includes changing the conditions of society that lead to economic disasters—for, make no mistake about it, such disasters are typically the result of some form of greed, as I relate below.

In any event—whether as Christians, members of other religions, or simply as ethical human beings—we should not take a passive stance to our world. In a subtle way, the Shemitah theory inclines people to do just that. This is one reason why we should toss it into the trash bin of failed theories.

Theories Like This Can Make Things Worse

Another problem with theories like the Shemitah theory is that they can become self-fulfilling 'prophecies.' Economists are becoming more aware that human psychology—the quirks of human thought, memory and emotion—is what actually drives the economy.[45] When people are discouraged about the future, they work less, they purchase less, they strive less—each of which acts to slow the economy down.

When the Dow Jones average plunged 777 points in a day on September 28, 2008—its worst point drop in history, up to this very day—the leader of one hedge fund sponsor summa-

---

[43] In the Bible: Matthew 25:31-46.
[44] In the Bible: James 1:27.
[45] For example, see Akerlof & Shiller (2010).

rized the situation succinctly: "This is a fear-driven market."[46] Emotions—hope, fear, panic—make a huge different in national and international economies.

We need to do better than be led to fear by empty, invalid theories. The current American economy is sluggish, but opportunities exist now that were virtually unthinkable ten years ago.[47] We need to mobilize our ingenuity and energy to deal with the challenges of the current environment. This cause is not furthered by attending to unsupported claims such as the Shemitah theory.

Why People Believe Claims Like This

It is worth trying to understand how people come to believe claims like the Shemitah theory in the first place. This can be a starting place for people to prepare themselves for the arrival of the next unfounded theory.

The Hardwired Guidelines of the Human Mind

Most Americans alive today were born since the end of the Second World War. For all of these people, the worst national economic catastrophe that they have witnessed was undoubtedly the Great Recession, which happened to go into its acute stage at the very end of the *Shemitah* year in the Fall of 2008. The aftermath was truly horrific: millions were thrown out of work, people's small businesses failed, and marriages crumbled under the ensuing stress. Of course, something this

---

[46]   Mark Groz, then of Topos LLC, quoted by K. Gibson (2008).

[47]   Publishing a book like this one in a print-on-demand edition and as an e-book is a good example of an opportunity unavailable a decade ago.

bad makes a vivid impression on the mind, and that memory will have a powerful emotional weight.

For any adult who has lived through the last seven years since the financial crisis went critical in September 2008, the notion of financial meltdown and economic catastrophe is certainly top of mind. Economics is the go-to concern for most American adults at present, overshadowing other concerns. When the Shemitah theory came to public awareness in 2014, with the publication of Mr. Cahn's *The Mystery of the Shemitah*, people already were primed to accept a future economic meltdown as probable. Why? Because of a peculiarity in the way that the human mind works.

People are not natural statisticians. Nonetheless, it is often necessary for people to make judgments about probabilities, because life is full of situations where we have to take action even in the presence of risk and uncertainty. What are the chances that I will be accepted to my top-choice school? What is the likelihood that I will be successful in Career A versus Careers B, C, or D? How much of a chance do I have with this attractive potential mate? How likely is it that I will be fired if I am a day late with completing this job at work? Is my child's illness basically nothing special, or should I be heading to the emergency room *right this very minute?* What are the chances that the money in my retirement account will vaporize over the next couple of years?

The human mind uses guidelines and shortcuts to make judgments about how likely it is that something is going to happen. These guidelines are known technically as *heuristics* (pronounced "hue-RIS-ticks"). The mind's heuristics often serve us well, but sometimes they lead us into the trap of mental bias as we make judgments. As two psychologists (one of them later a Nobel Award winner) explained it:

> There are situations in which people assess …
> the probability of an event by the ease with
> which instances or occurrences can be brought to
> mind. For example, one may assess the risk of
> heart attack among middle aged people by re-
> calling such occurrences among one's acquaint-
> ances…. This judgmental heuristic is called *avail-*
> *ability*…. [R]eliance on **[the] availability [heuris-**
> **tic]** leads to predictable biases.[48]

When people are still living in the aftermath of the largest economic crisis of the last half-century, of course they are primed to think that a future crisis is likely. Along comes the Shemitah theory, predicting economic crisis, and the human mind's availability heuristic makes it seem like this theory is more likely to be true than it actually is.

What we need to do to counteract the bias inherent in the availability heuristic is to assess ourselves honestly. We need to ask ourselves, does this idea appeal to me, maybe more than it actually should, because of what's happened to me in my life? An assessment like this would have caused a lot of people to look at the Shemitah theory with a more critical, even skeptical, eye.

There is another mental heuristic at work here, as well. When Mr. Cahn's book, *The Mystery of the Shemitah*, arrived in 2014, it came wrapped in the trappings of both scientific and religious respectability. There were charts and graphs, hall-marks of serious scholarship in economics. There were scrip-tural citations and discussions of biblical history, the sort of

---

[48]   Tversky & Kahneman (1974/2004) pp. 210-211, emphasis added.

thing we would expect in the work of a religious scholar. Mr. Cahn himself is the head of a congregation of Messianic Jewish Christians, which considers him both a rabbi and a pastor.

In short, the Shemitah theory had the trappings of plausibility. It thus activated another mental guideline that shapes human thought: **the representativeness heuristic**.[49] Simply put, the representativeness heuristic works by stereotypes; if something looks like a duck, it's probably a duck. If something appears to fit the stereotypical learned theory, then it probably is a valid theory—or so we think. But of course this heuristic can create problems, too. As the psychologists who first wrote about the representativeness heuristic put it:

> … this approach to the judgment of probability leads to serious errors because similarity, or representativeness, is not influenced by several factors which should affect judgments of probability.[50]

In other words, we need to go beyond surface appearances in judging the likelihood that something is what it appears to be. In the case of the Shemitah theory, we need to look at the details of the scriptural background, and the specifics of the claim and its purported statistical evidence. Then we see that surface appearances are misleading in this case.

Widespread Ignorance of the Specifics of the Bible

It is a matter of record that the general public is ignorant of the facts of the Bible's teachings, the facts of religious history, and the basics of religious belief—concerning their *own* re-

---

49   Tversky & Kahneman (1974/2004) pp. 203-204.
50   Tversky & Kahneman (1974/2004) p. 204.

ligions, let alone anybody else's. The religious studies professor Stephen Prothero has compiled much data from various sources documenting the fact that Americans are spectacularly uninformed about even their own religions. As he put it:

> Americans are both deeply religious and profoundly ignorant about religion. They are Protestants who can't name the four Gospels, Catholics who can't name the seven sacraments, and Jews who can't name the five books of Moses.... One of the most religious countries on earth is also a nation of religious illiterates.[51]

Indeed, Prothero points out that a measurable fraction of the American public believes that Joan of Arc is *Noah's wife!*

A 2010 survey by the Pew organization regarding religious knowledge in the United States revealed the following:

a. In a U.S. national survey of general religious knowledge using 32 questions, the overall average score was 16 correct. The highest scoring groups were atheists/agnostics, Jews, and Mormons (all averaging between 20 and 21 correct answers)— compared with Protestants (16 correct) and Catholics (14.7 correct).[52]

b. Specifically focusing on the 12 questions addressing the Bible and Christianity, the highest scoring group was the Mormons (average 7.9 correct), compared to any other group, including the general public (6.0 correct), Protestants as a whole (6.5 correct), White

---

[51]   Prothero (2007/2008) pp. 1-2.
[52]   *U.S. Religious Knowledge Survey* (2010), p. 6.

evangelical Protestants specifically (7.3 correct), and Catholics (5.4 correct). Jews scored an average of 6.3 correct, and atheists/agnostics an average of 6.7.[53]

Given that the overwhelming majority of believers in the United States are Protestants or Catholics, these findings don't speak well about the extent of biblical knowledge in the general American population. In this context, of course it would be predicted that relatively few Americans would have even heard about the sabbatical year in the Bible, let alone know its true meaning and application.

The implication here is clear: in order to evaluate theories that depend on the Bible, the reader must know and understand the biblical passages involved. There are abundant and reliable resources for self-education regarding the Bible and its interpretation. There is no excuse for people to be suckered into believing shaky theories supposedly based on the Bible.

What the Reader Can Do About the Risk of Economic Disruption

To Mr. Cahn, the economic disruptions that have accompanied some Shemitah years are judgments sent by God for the American people having abandoned His ways. If one holds such a point of view, the only thing one can do is repent, be more determined to follow God's ways, and try to minimize the discomfort for oneself and one's family.

As a Christian, I completely support the idea of repenting, better following God's ways, and preparing for hard times. But the same way that I would try to use plumbing tech rather than prayer alone to fix a leaky faucet, I recommend an utterly

---

[53] *U.S. Religious Knowledge Survey* (2010) p. 7.

different approach that Mr. Cahn's to dealing with the risk of economic disruption: **address its root causes**. Don't just worry about it, don't just complain about it, don't just pray about it—**work to fix it**. The root causes of America's current economic situation are not hard to find, and they are eminently fixable by a people determined to fix them.

Mr. Cahn's ideas to the contrary notwithstanding, financial crises, economic meltdowns, financial panics and so forth do not just descend from the sky like the fire that the Lord sent from heaven to consume the sacrifice prepared by the prophet Elijah.[54] Almost always, these economic problems occur because of human behavior.

Most such economic disruptions come about through one variety or another of greed. Wild speculation (in land, stocks, or commodities) makes certain investments very valuable; then the "bubble" in the value of the investments bursts, and fortunes are lost. Speculative investments are made in projects that offer little hope for paying back the investment. The wealthy use their influence to accumulate a greater proportion of the nation's wealth in fewer and fewer hands, leaving less purchasing power in the hands of the middle class, which is what drives a consumer economy such as our own.[55]

All of these problems are fixable. We can control wild speculation and the formation of bubbles through legislative oversight of stock, bond, and commodities markets. In a similar way, we can control investments in esoteric financial instruments (like "collateralized debt obligations") that are con-

---

[54]   In the Bible: 1 Kings 18: 30-39.

[55]   This point is eloquently made by Reich (2011) in relation to the current American economy.

fusing and unlikely to make a return to investors. We can pursue policies that will return purchasing power to the middle class.[56]

Why has this not already been done? Because, in the absence of an informed and involved electorate, money is what rules in the corridors of power. Becoming informed and being involved, of course, involves action, sustained over the course of years, rather than passively waiting for "someone to do something."

We are all children of God. But ultimately, God wants us to be *adults* of God. Adults work on their own problems. We need to do the same to deal with the root causes of economic disruption.

---

[56]   See Reich (2011), Part III, Chapters 1 and 2.

2

Wars and Rumors of Wars:
The Blood Moons Tetrad

Another of the most-frequently made claims about Fall 2015 is that this will be a period of world-shaking events, as supposedly foretold by the occurrence of the Four Blood Moons; below, I call this idea the Blood Moon Prophecy. In this chapter, I investigate these claims; explain why they are not true, but why people believe them anyway; and suggest what the reader might do to address the issues raised by the these claims, in a positive and productive way.

The Claims

Some have claimed that the occurrence of a group of four "Blood Moons" (total lunar eclipses), the last of which occurs on September 28, 2015, is a prelude to major events, including one or more of the following:

- A war involving the Jewish state of Israel. A major proponent of this idea is John Hagee, an American pastor who published these ideas in his 2013 book, *Four Blood Moons*.[57]

---

[57] Hagee (2013). See also Biltz (2014).

- The arrival of the Messiah. Proponents of this view, including some Jews,[58] point to the pronouncements of the ancient Jewish prophet Joel, regarding the "the great and terrible Day of the Lord." Christian proponents of this view also point to the teachings of Jesus regarding the circumstances surrounding his return to the Earth. Of course, for many Christians, the matter of the Second Coming of Christ raises the issue of the Rapture, as well (see below).

What Is True About Blood Moons

As with the Shemitah theory, there are some aspects of the claims about the 2014-2015 Blood Moon Tetrad that are true. Other aspects are false.

The Blood Moon Tetrad is an Actual Occurrence

During a total lunar eclipse, the Moon lies fully within the shadow of the Earth. (This always happens during the Full phase of the Moon, when it is exactly opposite the Sun from the perspective of the Earth.) During a total lunar eclipse, the moon can take on a reddish or coppery hue, as the light it receives from the Sun is refracted through the atmosphere of the Earth, which absorbs most other wavelengths of light but lets

---

[58] Adler (2015b). The arrival of the Messiah is also indicated, for some in the Jewish community, by the end of the Shemitah year in 2015, when considered in light of the so-called 'Bible Code' (Adler, 2015a). As I and my colleague Peter A. Hancock have suggested, the 'Bible Code' is fallacious (Hancock, 2007; Koltko-Rivera & Hancock, 2005).

red light through to the Moon. This is why the Moon during a total lunar eclipse can be called a "Blood Moon."

During the 21st century (January 1, 2001 through December 31, 2100), there have been or will be 85 total lunar eclipses.[59] Fourteen of these have occurred as of early September 2015; seventy-one more are yet to occur during the century.

There are also penumbral or partial lunar eclipses, when the Moon is only partially obscured by the shadow of the Earth. NASA scientist Fred Espenak notes that "when four consecutive lunar eclipses are all *total* eclipses, the group is known as a tetrad."[60] The lunar eclipses in tetrads occur approximately six months apart.[61]

A Blood Moon Tetrad Will Conclude During the Jewish Feast of Tabernacles in Late September 2015

The Blood Moon Tetrad of 2014-2015 consists of total lunar eclipses on the following dates,[62] all of which happen to be Jewish holidays, as noted:

- April 15, 2014: Passover

- October 8, 2014: Feast of Tabernacles

- April 4, 2015: Passover

- September 28, 2015: Feast of Tabernacles

For Tetrads to occur on Jewish holidays in this pattern is a rare occurrence.

---

59   Espenak (2003). See also "List of 21st-century lunar eclipses" (2015).
60   Espenak (2003), emphasis original.
61   Phillips (2014).
62   Espenak (2003); Espenak & Meeus (2011c).

There is Scriptural Precedent for the Idea that Blood Moons Precede Certain Major Events

At least 24 centuries ago, the ancient Jewish prophet Joel prophesied of a time he called "the Day of the Lord":

> Blow ye the trumpet in Zion, and sound an alarm in my holy mountain: let all the inhabitants of the land tremble: for the day of the Lord cometh, for it is nigh at hand; ...
>
> And I will shew wonders in the heavens and in the earth, blood, and fire, and pillars of smoke.
>
> The sun shall be turned into darkness, and the moon into blood, before the great and the terrible day of the Lord come.[63]

Four centuries later, the apostle Peter quoted Joel's words on the day of Pentecost.[64] "The Day of the Lord" is usually taken to mean the great destruction of God's enemies, and the redemption of His people, at the arrival of the Messiah (for Christians, the Second Coming).[65]

Jesus prophesied that before he returned to the Earth, there would be a terrible destruction in the land of Israel, including something called "the abomination of desolation."[66] Following that, he said, signs would appear in the heavens:

---

[63] In the Bible: Joel 2:1, 30-31.

[64] In the Bible: Acts 2:19-20.

[65] Dummelow (1908) p. 560.

[66] In the Bible: Matthew 24:15. The term "abomination of desolation" refers to the desecration of the Temple in Jerusalem. This occurred two centuries before Jesus, when, as foretold even earlier by the prophet

> Immediately after the tribulation of those days shall the sun be darkened, and the moon shall not give her light, and the stars shall fall from heaven, and the powers of the heavens shall be shaken:
>
> And then shall appear the sign of the Son of man in heaven: and then shall all the tribes of the earth mourn, and they shall see the Son of man coming in the clouds of heaven with power and great glory.[67]

It certainly seems that the idea of the Moon "turning to blood," spoken of in the scriptures, could refer to a total lunar eclipse, or Blood Moon, occurring before the great Day of the Lord. For Christians, the Day of the Lord would involve the Second Coming of Christ.

Many Christians also believe that the Second Coming occurs at or a few years after the Rapture, when, as many believe, true Christians will be caught up in the sky to meet

---

Daniel (see in the Bible: Daniel 11:31; 12:11), the Syrian king Antiochus Epiphanes and others plundered and profaned the Temple (see in the Apocrypha: 1 Maccabees 1:20-23, 54, 59). Other profanations of the Temple occurred over 30 years after Jesus' crucifixion, when the Zealots party among the Jews revolted against the Romans, took over the Temple area, and defiled it, as well as later, when the Roman emperor Titus then crushed the rebellion, desecrated the Temple with pagan worship, and then destroyed the Temple (Dummelow, 1908, p. 703).

Many Christians believe that the term also refers to a future time before the Second Coming, when the "man of sin" (the Antichrist) portrays himself as God in the Temple (see in the Bible: 2 Thessalonians 2:1-4); such Christians, of whom I am one, believe that Jesus will return to the Earth after this future profanation of the Temple.

[67]   In the Bible: Matthew 24:29-30.

Christ.[68] Thus, for some Christians, the idea of the Moon "turning to blood" is a sign to be given before the Rapture.

This is a Vulnerable Time for the State of Israel

It is true that, as many proponents of the Blood Moon Prophecy have pointed out, September 2015 is a particularly vulnerable time for the modern state of Israel. Here are the facts:

- In mid-September, Palestinians at the al-Aqsa mosque atop the Temple Mount in Jerusalem rained down rocks and debris onto Jewish worshipers engaged in prayer at the Western Wall. Efforts by the Israeli government to intervene at the mosque itself earned stern warnings from the government of Jordan.

---

[68]   In the Bible: 1 Thessalonians 4:16-17. Beliefs about the specifics of the Rapture differ sharply across Christian denominations. Some believe that the Rapture will simply involve the general resurrection at Christ's return; some think that believers will be caught up into the sky to meet Christ, and will then return to reign with him on Earth; some think that believers will be caught up to heaven, leaving non-believers to experience years of tribulation on Earth before the Second Coming. Some interpret the idea of the rapture figuratively.

Even Christians who believe in the literal Rapture vary widely in their opinions about the relationship between the Blood Moon Tetrad and the Rapture (cp. "Blood Moons – Tetrad Watch," 2015; *Red Moon Rapture,* n.d.), with some rejecting any such relationship entirely (e.g., Perkins, n.d.) John Hagee's position is that "the coming Four Blood Moons of 2014-2015 does *not* mean the Rapture is going to happen during that time. Why? Because the Rapture could happen at any moment" (Hagee, 2013, p. 242, italics added).

- The United Nations in New York City opened the 70th Session of the General Assembly on September 15th. The Annual General Debate, featuring speeches by many world leaders, will run from the 24th to the 30th of September (thus encompassing the date of the final Blood Moon in this Tetrad). One of the items of business that it is rumored will be debated at the General Assembly is a resolution recognizing a Palestinian state in what is now the Occupied Territories of the state of Israel.

- The likely endorsement in September by the United States Congress of "the Iran deal," which delays but does not stop nuclear development in Iran, is perceived by some to be a direct threat to the state of Israel.

Thus, there is unrest among the Palestinian population in Israel, the possibility of diplomatic developments that might increase that unrest, and a concern about a potential existential threat to the existence of the state of Israel—all occurring within the period of the current Blood Moon Tetrad. However, with the statement of these facts, the valid aspects of the Blood Moon Prophecy are exhausted.

Why the Blood Moon Prophecy Is Not True

Like the Shemitah theory, there are several ways in which the Blood Moon Prophecy fails. Here, too, we will first consider the historical record: over the history of the Jewish people, have Blood Moon Tetrads occurring on Passover and Sukkot (the Feast of Tabernacles) preceded trouble for the Jewish people, in terms of war or persecution? As we shall see, Blood Moon Tetrads have been very poor "signs" of such troubles.

Blood Moon Tetrads Have Not Predicted Problems for the Jewish People in the Past

John Hagee, a pastor who has had a major role in promoting the Blood Moon Prophecy, described his 'discovery' of the prophecy as follows:

> I began my search for answers to Pastor Mark [Biltz]'s challenging question, "Have you ever considered the sun, moon, and stars in the study of prophecy?" …
>
> … I just kept searching and could find nothing to validate the connection of the Four Blood Moons to prophecy. The Scriptures speak of "signs in the heavens," …. But still, I could not find the connection to prophecy. Then I thought for a moment and remembered my conversation with Pastor Mark; maybe these lunar signs are meant for Israel. God is the defender of Israel. He created Israel. Israel is His firstborn son (Exodus 4: 22). So I chose the first date that came to my mind, which was the year of Israel's rebirth, and typed in the following statement: "Total moon eclipse in 1948." What I saw in the middle of the computer screen made me literally leap out of my chair.
>
> Four "blood-red" total lunar eclipses will fall on Passover and Sukkot in 2014 and 2015, the

> same back-to-back occurrences at the time of
> 1492, 1949 and 1967.
>
> Those three dates were the most important dates
> in all of Israel's history![69] There have been sever-
> al Tetrads (four consecutive blood moons) since
> NASA first recorded their occurrences, but Tet-
> rads linked to significant Jewish history have
> happened only three times in more than five
> hundred years. These specific occurrences could
> not be ignored.[70]

Mr. Hagee might have done better by ignoring these specific occurrences of the Blood Moon Tetrads. This is because
they actually disprove his case.

The Tetrad did not predict the 1492 Edict of Expulsion.

It is true, as Mr. Hagee claims, that there was a Blood
Moon Tetrad in the years 1493-1494. The dates of the total lunar eclipses were as follows:

- April 2, 1493
- September 25, 1493
- March 22, 1494
- September 15, 1494[71]

---

[69] Of course, this is ludicrous. For the Jewish people, the dates of the
Abrahamic covenant, the exodus from Egypt, the Roman destruction
of the Temple and subsequent exile of the Jews, and the Holocaust, are
at least as important as anything else that Mr. Hagee mentions.

[70] Hagee (2013) pp. 169-171.

[71] Espenak & Meeus (2011a); "List of 15th-Century Lunar Eclipses"
(2015).

Mr. Hagee strongly emphasizes a supposed connection between this Tetrad and one of the catastrophic dates of Jewish history: the signing of the Edict of Expulsion by King Ferdinand and Queen Isabella of Spain. Signed on March 30, 1492, the order gave the Jews of Spain until August 1st to leave their kingdom, except for Jews who converted to the dominant Christian church of the time.

It is indisputably true that the Edict of Expulsion was a major and highly negative event in Jewish history. But the Blood Moon Tetrad of 1493-1494 cannot possibly have been a predictive sign of this horrible event, for one simple reason:

The Tetrad *followed* the Edict of Expulsion.

At the risk of mentioning the obvious, one would think that divine signs should *precede* the events of which they are signs.

What could possibly be the point of having a divine sign occur *after* a significant event that it is supposed to be associated with? I am quite sure that the Jews who had been expelled from Spain—the hundreds of thousands of Jews who were trudging or sailing off to other lands in Europe, Africa, the Near East, and even the New World, at the very time that the total lunar eclipses of this Tetrad were occurring—*were already quite sure that the Jews were in trouble!* And as for the tens of thousands of Jews still in Spain who were being tortured and even murdered, burned alive by the Spanish Inquisition, while the total lunar eclipses were happening—yes, I'm quite sure that they had been utterly convinced for some time that the Jews were in serious trouble!

If I had a house alarm that only went off long after my house had been burgled, I would not consider this at all useful. The Blood Moon Tetrad of 1493-1494 was completely useless from the perspective of prophecy.

The Tetrad Did Not Predict
the 1948 Israeli War of Independence.

It is true, as Mr. Hagee claims, that there was a Blood Moon Tetrad in the years 1949-1950. The dates of the total lunar eclipses were as follows:

- April 13, 1949

- October 7, 1949

- April 2, 1950

- September 26, 1950[72]

Mr. Hagee strongly emphasizes a supposed connection between this Tetrad and what is perhaps the most perilous time in the history of the state of Israel: the Israeli War of Independence, in which the Israelis fought off the combined armies of Egypt, Syria, and Jordan, as well as an expeditionary force from Iraq. The state of Israel had declared itself a nation on May 14, 1948; the following day, the Arab forces invaded, and the war was waged through March 10, 1949.

Again, it is indisputably true that, during the Israeli War of Independence, the existence of the Jewish state of Israel hung in the balance, the sword of destruction suspended above it by a thin and fraying thread. However, the Blood Moon Tetrad of 1949-1950 cannot possibly have been a predictive sign of this high-stakes event, for a reason that, by now, I

---

[72] Espenak & Meeus (2011b); "List of 20th-Century Lunar Eclipses" (2015).

am sure readers can identify for themselves: the Tetrad *followed* the entire war, from outbreak through conclusion. Here again, one really expects that a true divine sign would precede the event of which it is a signal.

In all fairness, Mark Biltz—who seems to have been the first to have discovered the 'connection' between the Blood Moon Tetrad, the Jewish holidays, and Jewish history—has responded to criticisms like this. As he has written:

> Some readers say the eclipses are irrelevant because one time a significant event might come *after* the four blood moons, and another time it might occur *before* them. This is also totally missing the point. Think of it this way: America or the United Nations may think that they should get the credit (or blame, depending on how you look at it) for creating Israel in 1948, but the fact that these four blood moons occurred in 1949 and 1950 is, I believe, God's way of telling the world it was His doing and had nothing to do with the United Nations! They were mere puppets in the hand of God! In 1967, when the first of the four blood moons occurred a few months before the Six-Day War, God was telling the nation of Israel that His hands were going to be all over it. Sadly, these signals were totally missed by everyone anyway, as the connections were not made until I discovered them in 2008. At

least this time we have a forewarning of what may come![73]

No, we don't. We do *not* have a forewarning of what may come. And critics of the Blood Moon Prophecy are *not* missing the point when they say that the Blood Moons are irrelevant for the reasons stated. Although I do not believe that Mr. Biltz realizes what he has done, in the passage above, he both slants the facts and changes the whole meaning that he says the Blood Moon Tetrad has.

First of all, it is not the case that "one time a significant event might come *after* the four blood moons, and another time it might occur *before* them." Mr. Biltz, like Mr. Hagee and others, believe that previous Blood Moon Tetrads were associated with three major events in Jewish history: the Edict of Expulsion from Spain in 1492, the Israeli War of Independence in 1948, and the Israeli Six-Day War in 1967. As I have documented above, the first two events occurred before the Blood Moon Tetrads that were supposedly associated with them. Only the Six-Day War provides the slightest support for the idea that a Tetrad might presage a significant event, and even in that event, only the first Blood Moon of the Tetrad occurred before the war itself.[74] Blood Moon Tetrads, in whole or in part, always seem to *follow* the events they are supposedly associated with. They don't "forewarn" us of anything at all.

Secondly, Mr. Biltz is shifting the ground where the supposed 'meaning' of the Blood Moon Tetrads is concerned. At

---

[73] Biltz (2014) pp. 158-159.

[74] The Arab-Israeli Six-Day War took place from June 4th through June 10, 1967. The four Blood Moons of the Tetrad took place on April 24th and October 18th of 1967, and April 13th and October 6th of 1968 (Espenak & Meeus, 2011b).

the end of the passage, he talks of the signs "forewarning" us (which they don't). But the main body of his passage claims that the point of the Blood Moon Tetrad on Jewish holidays is for God to send a special message that God has the circumstances under control, that everything is following God's plan. It is as if God is saying, "I've got this," to Mr. Biltz.

Really? How about every other year in the history of humanity? Does God *not* have the circumstances under control?

In addition, what kind of cruel sign is it that people don't even get to see until generations, or centuries, after the event involved? If the Blood Moon Tetrad of the late 15th century was supposed to be of any comfort to the Jews being exiled or tortured—well, *that* was a great big fail, as no one knew about it until Mr. Biltz 'discovered' it over 5 centuries later!

So are these supposed 'signs' just supposed to be instructional for *our* generation, in the 21st century? Why would we need those signs? Anyone who does not already believe the Bible as God's word is not going to suddenly be convinced of God's power by the Blood Moon Prophecy. And anyone who believes the Bible is already convinced of God's power.

In sum, the Blood Moon Tetrads are useless as predictive signs, and unnecessary as signals of God's presence in human history. However, there is another, far more horrifying, way in which the Blood Moon Tetrads have failed God's people.

The Tetrad utterly failed to warn the Jews of the Holocaust.

The greatest failure of the Tetrad-as-divine-sign idea, however, involves another matter altogether: the worst catastrophe to hit the Jewish people since at least as far back as the destruction of their Temple by the Romans, nearly twenty centuries ago. I speak, of course, of the Holocaust, the murder of six million Jews, comprising one-third of all the Jews in the world at the time, all destroyed by forces loyal to Adolf Hitler, during the span of only 12 years in the early 20ᵗʰ century.

Hitler became the Chancellor of Germany on January 30, 1933. This date effectively marks the definitive seizing of power in Germany by the Nazi Party. Later that year, the first laws discriminating against Jews in professions and agriculture were passed in Germany. On *Kristallnacht*, "Crystal Night," the evening of November 9-10, 1938, riots organized by the Nazis throughout Germany and Austria smashed the windows of Jewish businesses and synagogues; 30,000 Jews were arrested and sent (temporarily) to concentration camps, and over a thousand synagogues were burned.

Germany invaded Poland—whose population included three million Jews—on September 1, 1939, which began the Second World War in Europe. Organized murders of Jews began in Poland that year. Mass killings of Jews were instituted in Nazi-occupied territories in Poland and the Soviet Union. By 1942, half a dozen Nazi death camps for Jews had been established in occupied Poland. On January 20, 1942, at a 90-minute conference of Nazi senior officers held at the Berlin suburb of Wannsee, Nazi leaders made plans to coordinate their actions so as to efficiently transfer all Jews throughout Europe to death camps in the eastern territories, such as Poland. These efforts continued at full steam right up until the defeat of the Nazi regime in the spring of 1945.

What did the Blood Moon Tetrads have to say about any of this? Nothing. ˚

From January 30, 1933 (the date when Hitler and the Nazis came to power) through April 30, 1945 (the reported date of Hitler's suicide), no Tetrad of Blood Moons occurred. (A Tetrad did occur during 1927-1928; there was no further Tetrad until 1949-1950.)

What kind of supposed divine sign of danger for the Jewish people "misses" the worst conceivable event for the Jews—mass extermination—to occur over the last 20 centuries? This failure alone is reason sufficient to reject the idea that a Tetrad of Blood Moons is such a sign.

As I said earlier with regard to the Shemitah theory, perhaps the most powerful refutation of a claim is to show that it is false, even using the same assumptions that the claim itself uses. As with the Shemitah theory, the most important assumption for the Blood Moon Prophecy is that the Bible is the word of God. Even working from that basis, the Blood Moon Prophecy lacks support.

There Is No Scriptural Basis for Tetrads as Signs

As with the Shemitah theory, there is no way to say this nicely, so I shall state it bluntly yet again. Everyone who claims that a Tetrad of Blood Moons is some kind of divine sign of trouble for Jews is just making this up. *There is not a shred of scriptural evidence that a Tetrad of Blood Moons is to be considered something special in the way of a divine sign.*

Does the Bible state that the Day of the Lord will be preceded by the Moon "turning to blood"? Sure it does, as I have documented above. Could this mean the occurrence of a Blood Moon? Sure it could. But it is a very great leap from saying that *some* total lunar eclipse, at *some* time, will precede that Great and Terrible Day, to saying that a group of *four* such lunar eclipses—even those occurring on Passovers and Sukkot festivals—have some special meaning for the Jewish people. Such a claim occurs nowhere in the Bible, nor in Jewish traditional literature that has accumulated over the course of many centuries (such as the Talmud or the Zohar).

The same thing applies to the idea of the Second Coming of Christ. Did Jesus say that his return would be preceded by the Moon "turning to blood"? Of course. And, yes, this could certainly be a total lunar eclipse. But there is nothing at all in the Bible to say that a Blood Moon Tetrad is a sign, even if it occurs during special Jewish holidays.

So, yet again, as with the Shemitah theory, neither the facts of history nor the actual words of scripture provide any support for the Blood Moon Prophecy. And again, when confronted with this yawning gap in support for said Prophecy, the most sensible thing for people to do is to just ignore the Blood Moon Tetrads as signs, and focus on addressing their real-life concerns in effective ways.

Why This All Matters

As with the Shemitah theory, the reader might well ask, why is it necessary to bury the Blood Moon Prophecy so deeply? There is a very good reason to do so.

The Blood Moon Prophecy Is Being Used to Validate All Sorts of Bizarre Claims

It is not enough for some people to say that the Blood Moon Tetrads are divine signs of forthcoming wars involving the Jews. The Blood Moon Prophecy is being used as *evidence*—as if were valid in the first place—to support a pile of other claims, ranging from the merely misguided to the frankly nutty. During the period between the end of the Shemitah year (September 13, 2015) and the fourth and last of the Blood Moons in the current Tetrad (September 28, 2015), a number of events are occurring that some people are giving special attention to—precisely *because* they fall within this especially charged period. These events, and the myths being spun around them, include the following[75]:

- Sept. 23: Pope Francis, the 266th Pope, meets with the President of the United States on the 266th day of the year. Wait a minute! The average gestation time for a human child is 266 days! *Is something being 'birthed' at this meeting?* Could it be the birth of the New World Order? *The rise of the Antichrist?*[76]

- Sept. 25: This is the 500th day following the May 14, 2014 statement by French Foreign Minister Laurent Fabius' statement that the world had 500 days to avert "climate chaos."[77] Could it be that Mr. Fabius let slip knowledge being kept from the public, perhaps about a climate catastrophe that will be produced by comet or meteor strikes—perhaps pro-

---

[75] Events are largely selected from the list provided by Snyder (2015). The myth descriptions are largely my own.

[76] For the supposed New World Order connection to this meeting, see Price (2015). The conjunction of the papal visit with the Blood Moon is prominently featured in some online statements equating either the Pope or the President with the Antichrist, e.g., SignsofThyComing (2014). See also cloudbase rapture (2015).

[77] My guess is that Mr. Fabius meant that there were only 500 days until the U.N.'s Sustainable Development Summit, which does begin on September 25, as I describe below.

voked by the gravitational influence of the star Nemesis, or the Planet Nibiru?[78]

- Sept. 25-27: The United Nations holds its Sustainable Development Summit,[79] which over 150 world leaders are expected to attend. The point of this meeting is to formally adopt *Transforming Our World: The 2030 Agenda for Sustainable Development*, which focuses on ending poverty through sustainable economic development. In the conspiracist community, this is being touted as a major step towards one-world government and the loss of national sovereignty.[80] (The draft document is available online.[81] Readers can decide for themselves just how malignant goals like ending "poverty and hunger" are.)

- Could the Messiah be arriving in September, given this unusual sequence of the end of a Shemitah year followed by the fourth Blood Moon in the Tetrad?[82]

---

[78] Styxhexenhammer666 (2015) ridicules a group of such theories. There is no scientific support for the existence of either the star Nemesis or the Planet Nibiru.

[79] *United Nations Sustainable Development Summit 2015* (2015).

[80] E.g., Breaking Truth (2015), John Birch Society (2015).

[81] United Nations (2015).

[82] As one reporter put it:

> … the blood moon this Sukkot will occur just two weeks after the end of the current Shemitah year. This is significant because the Talmud, the most important collection of rabbinic teachings in Judaism, suggests that the messiah will come in the year following a Shemitah year. (Adler, 2015)

- Could the recently upgraded and reactivated Large Hadron Collider at CERN destroy the world sometime in September — perhaps by actually opening a portal to Hell?[83]

Okay, then: we have the birth of a devilish plan and/or the Antichrist, the opening of a gate to Hell, the arrival of the Messiah, the destruction of the world — wow, September 2015 is going to be one busy month! And belief in these bizarre theories is empowered and facilitated by the belief that the Blood Moon Tetrad is some sort of divine sign.

Why People Believe Claims Like This

In the preceding chapter, I mentioned biblical ignorance as a reason that people fall for ideas like the Shemitah theory, and biblical ignorance is just as powerful an influence on belief in the Blood Moon Prophecy. I also mentioned two heuristics, or mental guidelines, that sometimes bias people into giving greater credence to ideas than they should. The same heuristics apply to belief in the Blood Moon Prophecy.

The availability heuristic certainly applies here. The United States has been in a continual state of armed conflict since October 2001, when it attacked Afghanistan in response to the 9-11 attacks. That is almost 14 years of war, still ongoing, in Afghanistan, Iraq, and elsewhere. With Russia's annexation of Crimea, and its armed actions in the east of Ukraine, along with threats of attack from North Korea, and expansionist activities by China, war is a keen subject in the news. Conse-

---

[83] "Top scientists issue huge alert: Everything in place to open gates of Hell this year — 2015" (2015).

quently, for many Americans, war and all its consequences are never far from their thoughts. In this context, the idea of some sort of divine sign of forthcoming war certainly seems plausible: this is the availability heuristic at work.

The representativeness heuristic applies here as well. The Blood Moon Prophecy comes wrapped in the language of the Bible: Jewish holidays that have been observed for thousands of years; prophecies of signs in the sky by ancient prophets, apostles of Jesus, and Jesus himself. In this context, the Blood Moon Prophecy seems plausible—more plausible than it actually is, because of the representativeness heuristic guiding our thoughts.

With the Blood Moon Tetrad, however, an additional aspect of human psychology comes into play. One of the most important cognitive skills that human beings possess is *pattern recognition*. This is what enables human beings to notice weather patterns, predict where minerals will be found, diagnose illnesses, even detect the presence of serial killers. It can be said that the brain is a sort of machine for pattern recognition. So strongly does the brain focus on pattern recognition that it *creates* patterns in totally random stimuli; this is what the brain does as we see patterns in clouds, or in the grain of pieces of wood, or in inkblots on a page.

The tendency to see patterns can reach extremes in psychotic individuals. Perhaps the best media example of this is the character played by Jim Carrey in the 2007 film, *The Number 23*: as the character descends further into madness, he sees the number 23—as well as its multiples and permutations—show up in more and more contexts and malevolent connections. But one does not have to be psychotic to have one's capacity for pattern recognition run amok.

People are "seeing" a pattern that does not really exist, in the supposed connection between Blood Moon Tetrads and world events. Given that people have the *capacity* to do this—being pattern-recognizing creatures—why *would* they? I believe it is because we live in a complex world with frightening possibilities. To see patterns is to obtain some control over the situation. Even if the pattern is unreal, the subjective feeling of control is somewhat comforting.

But this sense of control is nothing but an illusion. If we want to actually exert some control over the complex world we live in, we must take action in the real world.

What the Reader Can Do

As with the Shemitah theory, the thing to do with the Blood Moon Prophecy is to discard it, and to take action that might make a difference in the real world. This applies equally well to each of the two main issues that are typically associated with the Blood Moon Tetrad: the welfare of the Jewish people, and the arrival of the Messiah.

The Welfare of the Jewish People

The Jewish people face threats both from within and without. Anti-Semitism is on the rise everywhere, and armed attacks on Jews have become such a concern in Europe that, reportedly, 70% of European Jews conceal their religion, and only 15% plan to attend synagogue during the 2015 High Holidays.[84] Anti-Semitic rhetoric is certainly on the rise, as evidenced by the support given to a news commentator's anti-Jewish Twitter tweet,[85] as well as the credence still given around the world to the virulently anti-Semitic *Protocols of the Elders of Zion*.[86] The physical security of Israel is continually in danger. Globally, assimilation is a continual issue, as is the nurturing of Jewish identity in the younger generation.

But these are things that people, **both Jews and others**, can do something about. For example:

- We can educate ourselves about such libels as the *Protocols of the Elders of Zion*, and vigorously oppose their propagation as depictions of the truth on every occasion when the subject arises.

- We can show no tolerance for the scapegoating of Jews as such statements show up in public discourse.

- We can promote Jewish education, and participate in it ourselves, either through formal instruction, or self-study.

- We can encourage American governmental policies that lend support to the state of Israel.

- We can promote productive solutions for the security and well-being of the Palestinian population in Israel, which is both a moral impera-

---

84 Weiss & Brackman (2015).

85 Shire (2015).

86 Sokol (2015). The amazing yet horrifying story of the libel of the *Protocols*, and their pernicious influence, is told by Cohn (1967/2005) and Eisner (2005), the latter in the form of a graphic novel.

tive and a key to long-term security for the Jewish state.

Preparation for the Arrival of the Messiah

There is no point to anxiety about the arrival of the Messiah (whether one thinks of this in terms of the appearance of
the Jewish Messiah, or the Second Coming of Christ). No one
can make it happen sooner, or delay it.

The one thing—the *only* thing—over which a human being can exert control about this issue is the matter of one's
own preparation for that arrival. That preparation involves
one's personal spirituality, one's orientation towards God and
God's laws (however one understands them).

There are many aspects to personal spirituality. There are
such dimensions as ethical behavior, prayer and contempla-
tion, study, ritual observance, communal worship, and partic-
ipation in a community. I am sure that each of us can find
some aspect of our personal spirituality that could stand improvement; most of us, such as myself, need improvement in
several areas.

This is how to deal with the approach of the Messiah: to
strive to *always* be ready. Then, it really won't matter when the
Messiah arrives.

3

Concluding Thoughts:
On Unusual Claims

We have covered a lot of ground together, for such a brief book. I shall leave the reader with several concluding thoughts about how to respond when hearing an unusual or sensationalistic theory.

1. Remember that extraordinary claims require extraordinary proof

It is said that the astronomer and educator Carl Sagan promoted a powerful guideline: "Extraordinary claims require extraordinary proof." Accept no one's word for anything: not a scientist's, not a religious leader's, not a scholar's, most certainly not an anonymous source's, or a vague source such as "they say." Find out the facts—the *facts*, not the rumors!—and evaluate them for yourself.

2. Know the scriptural background involved

Many unusual claims say that they are based on the Bible. As I have documented in Chapter 1, most Americans' knowledge of the Bible is singularly unimpressive. Yet the Bible is available in a panoply of editions, priced for every budget (including free on the Internet). Before you give some of your mental real estate over to a theory that claims biblical support, make the effort to learn what the Bible actually says about the topic.

Be aware that there are a variety of approaches that one can take to the Bible, and make a considered decision about which one applies to the situation at hand.[87] Don't fall prey to someone's theory, just because they seem to have read more in the Bible than you have.

3. Know (and check) the facts and the logic

Does someone say that such-and-such is a sign of this and that? Check the *historical* background and see whether that makes sense. Does someone say that 'scientists have found' such-and-such a controversial phenomenon? Check out the *scientific* background and see whether that makes sense. And for any claim, check out the *logic* involved.[88]

7. Keep your biases in check

I have pointed out three biases that the human mind is prone to: the malfunctions of, respectively, the availability heuristic, the representativeness heuristic, and the mind's pattern recognition function. There are others, of course, some of

---

[87] For example, to understand the biblical book of Revelation (also known as the Apocalypse of St. John), it is helpful to know of the four major approaches that people have taken to this text: see Clegg (1997).

[88] Extreme example: People who claim that the Pope is a member of the Illuminati, or that the Illuminati are Satanists, have quite a set of logical leaps to explain—given that the historical Bavarian Illuminati were anticlerical atheists, and the movement was dead as a doornail by the late 18th century (Hodapp & Von Kannon, 2008; Melanson, 2009).

them quite powerful, especially including in-group prejudice (based on race, ethnicity, religion, nationality, or locale) and the tendency to put our own selves in the best possible light.

This is perhaps the hardest of my recommendations to carry out, for most people. But learning to recognize the limitations of one's own mind and background is an important part of becoming a mature human being. This all may mean confronting harsh truths about ourselves, our behavior, even our beliefs. But, as it is written, "the truth will set you free."[89]

---

[89] In the Bible: John 8:32.

Appendix

The Shemitah Theory:
A Statistical Analysis

The Shemitah cycle is a 7-year cycle, originally applied to agricultural efforts among the ancient Hebrews; every seventh year is designated as the Shemitah, a sabbatical year.[90] It has been hypothesized that the years of the seven-year Shemitah cycle differ in their stock market outcomes. Specifically, according to the financial manager Thomas Pound, "the theory … states that every seven years, there is the potential for a market calamity."[91] Pound bases this hypothesis on the work of Jonathan Cahn, who has appeared in print and online concerning the Shemitah economic disaster hypothesis.[92]

The present study tested the Shemitah economic disaster hypothesis using data from the American stock market stretching back to the later 19th century through the year 2008.

Method

The years of the Shemitah cycle were defined first by using the cycle as implemented in the present-day state of Isra-

---

[90] "Shmita" (2015).
[91] Pound (2015).
[92] Cahn (2014).

el.[93] Thus, following current usage in the state of Israel, it was determined that the Jewish year beginning in the Fall season of Gregorian year 2001 (and thus ending in the Fall of 2002) was the first year of a Shemitah cycle, and the Jewish year beginning in the Fall season of Gregorian year 2007 (and thus ending in the Fall of 2008) was the seventh, or Shemitah, year of that same cycle.

For years previous to the Jewish calendar year 5712 (Gregorian year 1951-1952), which saw the first observance of the Shemitah year in the modern state of Israel, the calendar scheme in current use in that state was extrapolated backwards into the later 19th Century. In this manner, it was determined that the Jewish year beginning in the Fall season of Gregorian year 1875 (and thus ending in the Fall of Gregorian year 1876) was the first year of a Shemitah cycle, and that the Jewish year beginning in the Fall of Gregorian year 1881 (and thus ending in the Fall of Gregorian year 1882) was the seventh, or Shemitah, year of that same cycle.

Data regarding stock market prices were taken from Robert Shiller's database, "U.S. Stock Markets 1871-Present and CAPE Ratio," available on his website.[94] The database lists the closing Standard and Poor's (S&P) Composite index as of the last day of the month, for every month from January 1871 through August 2015 (as of the time of the present study).

We used year-end data for the S&P Composite for each Gregorian year from 1875 through 2008. The thought here was that, if the Shemitah year is a true sign of forthcoming losses in the market, those losses should become apparent in the

---

[93] "Shmita" (2015).

[94] "Online Data Robert Shiller" (n.d.).

three-to-four-month period between the conclusion of the Shemitah year, by the Jewish calendar, and the conclusion of the corresponding Gregorian year (hereafter called the "Gregorian Shemitah year").

For each Gregorian year from 1872 through 2014, I calculated the year-end percentage gain or loss in the S&P for the year, compared to the preceding Gregorian year. I used these gain/loss data as the dependent variable in my statistical analyses. For the analysis of variance (ANOVA) described below, I only used data from the years 1876 -2008, which comprise 19 complete Shemitah cycles of 7 years apiece.

The statistical model that I chose to apply to the data involved treating each seven-year Shemitah cycle as an individual "subject" in a repeated-measures ANOVA design, wherein the year-end S&P percentage gains and losses constituted seven "scores" per subject; the seven groups in the design are thus defined by the seven years of each cycle, across 19 cycles. This kind of model is in keeping with the view that each Shemitah cycle is separate unto itself, which seems to underlie the literature supporting the Shemitah economic disaster hypothesis.

That said, I realize that the current situation does not actually meet the assumptions of a repeated-measures ANOVA design. Strictly speaking, for such a design to be valid, each subject in the study would have to be selected, and then perform, completely independently of all other subjects.[95] That is clearly not the case here: It would be ludicrous to expect that the market performance of one economic cycle (however defined) would somehow not depend at all on the previous economic cycle, or that it would not affect to some degree the performance of the subsequent iteration of the economic cycle.

---

[95]   B. H. Cohen (2008) p. 505.

However, my thought was to test the Shemitah stock market hypothesis on its own terms, as it were, even at the risk of stacking the statistical deck in its favor.

Results

The distribution of the S&P gain/loss data by year of the Shemitah cycle (Year 1 through Year 7, across all complete and partial Shemitah cycles) was approximately normal for each of the seven 'year groups.' While checking these distributions, I found that of the 20 instances of Gregorian Shemitah years during this period, in 7 cases (35%), the S&P showed a gain during the year. For Gregorian Shemitah years that showed a gain, the median gain in the S&P was 15.2% over the course of the year. This is interesting in light of the apparently widespread perception in some circles that Shemitah years are harbingers of economic disaster.

A one-way repeated measures ANOVA was conducted to evaluate the null hypothesis that there is no difference in percent changes in the Standard & Poor's index across the seven years of the Shemitah cycle (N = 19). The results of the ANOVA indicated a marginally statistically significant year effect, Wilks's Lambda = 0.429, $F(6, 13) - 2.889$, $p = .051$, $\eta^2 = .571$. The sample size was too small to obtain sufficient power; observed power = .697. Thus, these results were equivocal regarding the appropriateness of rejecting the null hypothesis.

Follow-up comparisons indicated that no pairwise difference was significant at the $p \leq .05$ level. Thus, there was no statistically significant difference across years of the Shemitah cycle in terms of percent changes in the S&P index against the preceding year.

Discussion

One of the more prominent proponents of the Shemitah economic disaster hypothesis has stated that the Shemitah is to be understood as "a prophetic sign—particularly as a warning or manifestation of national judgment,"[96] especially as reflected in economic distress. The findings of the present study do not lend any support to the idea that the conclusion of a Shemitah year is some kind of divine harbinger or "sign" of economic trouble to come in the stock market.

It could be argued that the present study was not a fair test of the Shemitah stock market hypothesis, because it only included data from 19 economic cycles. This is a valid criticism, given that the observed power in the present study is so low (observed power = .697, while recommended minimum power = .800). As the late Jacob Cohen pointed out, in an analogous situation involving a one-way independent groups ANOVA, it would require about 32 subjects per group in each of 7 groups to reach a power of .80, assuming a medium effect size and a conventional predetermined significance level.[97] It is thus recommended that this study be repeated in approximately the year 2099, when data shall be available from an additional 13 Shemitah cycles.

In the meantime, it should be pointed out that, given all the hype in the popular press concerning the supposedly dire outlook portended by the end of a Shemitah year, it would be expected that the observed effect size if the hypothesis were true would be in the large range, not the medium. As Cohen noted, for the analogous situation of a one-way independent groups ANOVA, we would expect to need only 13 subjects in

---

[96] Cahn (2014), p. 55.

[97] J. Cohen (1992) p. 158.

each of seven groups, to detect a large effect size.[98] The present study had more than this number of subjects per year group (N = 19). In sum, the results of the current study do not provide any support for the Shemitah economic disaster hypothesis.

---

[98]   J. Cohen (1992) p. 158.

References

Citations in the footnotes of this book which display two dates separated by a slash (such as "Tversky & Kahneman, 1974/2004") were originally published on the earlier date but reprinted in a new edition on the later date. They are found in the References section under the *later* date.

Adler, R. L. (2015a, July 8). Bible codes hint to arrival of Messiah after end of Shemitta year [online news article]. *Breaking Israel News*. Retrieved September 13, 2015 from http://www.breakingisraelnews.com/44778/bible-codes-hint-arrival-messiah-after-shmitta-year-jewish-world

Adler, R. L. (2015b, July 31). Upcoming blood moon to lead to "Messianic advancement" [online news article]. *Breaking Israel News*. Retrieved September 13, 2015, from http://www.breakingisraelnews.com/46098/upcoming-blood-moon-messianic-advancement-jewish-world

Akerlof, G. A., & Shiller, R. J. (2010). *Animal spirits: How human psychology drives the economy, and why it matters for global capitalism*. Princeton, NJ: Princeton University Press.

Aum Shinrikyo [online encyclopedia article]. Retrieved May 15, 2011 from http://en.wikipedia.org/wiki/Aum_Shinrikyo

Berkowitz, A. E. (2015, September 1). Mathematician: Shmittah market trends point to "really bad" crash in September [online news article]. *Breaking Israel News: Latest News, Biblical Perspective* [website]. Retrieved September 14, 2015 from http://www.breakingisraelnews.com/48068/shmittah-market-trends-point-to-really-bad-crash-in-september

Bilton, N. (2015, October). Unicorns and rain clouds. *Vanity Fair*, issue no. 662, pp. 168, 170, 173, 174, 177.

Biltz, M. (2014). *Blood Moons: Decoding the imminent heavenly signs*. Washington, DC: WND Books.

Biographical sketch [: Robert J. Shiller]. (n.d.). Retrieved September 15, 2015 from http://www.econ.yale.edu/~shiller/bio.htm

Blood Moons – Tetrad watch [web page]. (2015). *Rapture Watch: A Global End Times Prophecy Resource*. Retrieved September 17, 2015 from http://www.rapturewatch.net/blood-moons-tetrad

Breaking Truth. (2015, August 19). Warning! Global government imminent! Agenda 2030, TTIP, TPA, & TPP [online video]. Viewed September 18, 2015 at https://www.youtube.com/watch?v=TSCKW2rS8_I

Cahn, J. (2014). *The mystery of the Shemitah*. Lake Mary, FL: Frontline / Charisma Media.

Campbell, A., & Sanderson, B. (2011, May 13). The end of the world! Doomsayer puts $140,000 into his May 21 prediction. *New York Post*, p. 14.

Clarke, T. (2014, February 13). Stock market crash history: The Dow's 10 biggest one-day plunges [online news article]. *Money Morning*. Retrieved September 10, 2015, from http://moneymorning.com/2014/02/13/stock-market-crash-history-dows-10-biggest-one-day-plunges/

Clegg, S. (Ed.). (1997). *Revelation: Four views: A parallel commentary*. Nashville, TN: Thomas Nelson Publishers.

cloudbase rapture.(2015, May 14). Birth of the Antichrist Obama as foretold in the Blood Red Moons 19th century

[online video]. Viewed September 17, 2015 at
https://www.youtube.com/watch?v=j99c-G0viTc

Cohen, B. H. (2008). *Explaining psychological statistics* (3rd ed.).
Hoboken, NJ: Wiley.

Cohen, J. (1992). A power primer. *Psychological Bulletin, 112,*
155-159.

Cohn, N. (2005). *Warrant for genocide: The myth of the Jewish
world conspiracy and the* Protocols of the Elders of Zion.
London, England: Serif. (Original work published 1967)

Dummelow, J. R. (1908). *A commentary on the Holy Bible.* New
York, NY: Macmillan.

"Edgar C. Whisenant" [online encyclopedia article]. Retrieved
September 10, 2015 from https://en.wikipedia.org/wiki/
Edgar_C._Whisenant

Eisner, W. (2005). *The Plot: The secret story of the Protocols of the
Elders of Zion.* New York, NY: Norton.

Espenak, F. (2003, September 11). *Lunar eclipses: 2001 to 2100*
[web page]. Retrieved September 16, 2015 from
http://web.archive.org/web/20070305183925/http://sunearth
.gsfc.nasa.gov/eclipse/LEcat/LE2001-2100.html

Espenak, F., & Meeus, J. (2011a). Five millennium catalog of
lunar eclipses – 1401 to 1500 (1401 CE to 1500 CE) [web
page]. *NASA eclipse web site.* Retrieved September 18, 2015
from http://eclipse.gsfc.nasa.gov/LEcat5/LE1401-1500.html

Espenak, F., & Meeus, J. (2011b). Five millennium catalog of
lunar eclipses – 1901 to 2000 (1901 CE to 2000 CE) [web
page]. *NASA eclipse web site.* Retrieved September 18, 2015
from http://eclipse.gsfc.nasa.gov/LEcat5/LE1901-2000.html

Espenak, F., & Meeus, J. (2011c). Five millennium catalog of
lunar eclipses – 2001 to 2100 (2001 CE to 2100 CE) [web

page]. *NASA eclipse web site*. Retrieved September 18, 2015 from http://eclipse.gsfc.nasa.gov/LEcat5/LE2001-2100.html

Gibson, K. (2008, September 29). U. S. stocks hammered after House rejects rescue [online news story]. *MarketWatch*. Retrieved September 17, 2015 from http://www.marketwatch.com/story/us-stocks-slide-dow-plunges-777-points-as-bailout-bill-fails-2008929164700

Goffard, C. (2011, May 21). Harold Camping is at the heart of a mediapocalypse. *Los Angeles Times* [online edition]. As of May 21, 2011, available at http://www.latimes.com/news/local/la-me-rapture-20110521,0,5053003.story

Graves, N., & Alpert, L. I. (2011, May 13). Adman for the end of days. *New York Daily News*, p.14.

Hancock, P. A. (2007). A many-headed Hydra: Reason for the persistence of the 'Bible Code' and suggested anodynes [online scholarly paper]. *Skeptical Briefs, 17*(3). Retrieved September 17, 2015 from http://www.csicop.org/sb/show/many-headed_hydra_reasons_for_the_persistence_of_the_bible_code_and_suggest/

Hagee, J. (2013). *Four Blood Moons*. Brentwood, TN: Worthy Publishing/Worthy Media.

Heald, S. (2011, May 13). Doomsday will come not on May 21 but as a slow burner. *The Washington Post* [online edition]. Available at http://www.washingtonpost.com/opinions/doomsday-will-come-not-on-may-21-but-as-aslow-burner/2011/05/06/AFthWz2G_story.html

Hodapp, C., & Von Kannon, A. (2008). *Conspiracy theories and secret societies for dummies*. Hoboken, NJ: Wiley.

Hohmann, L. (2015a, September 1). Statistician: Data proves biblical financial collapse [online news article]. *WND*. Retrieved September 10, 2015 from http://www.wnd.com/2015/09/statistician-data-proves-shemitah-financial-collapse/

Hohmann, L. (2015b, September 12). 'Strange signs' on Shemitah's final days [online news article]. *WND*. Retrieved September 12, 2015 from http://www.wnd.com/2015/09/strange-signs-on-shemitahs-final-days/

High-level meetings of the 70th session (2015) [web page]. (2015). Retrieved September 17, 2015 from http://www.un.org/en/ga/70/meetings/

Holmes, D. L. (2006). *The faiths of the founding fathers*. New York, NY: Oxford University Press.

The John Birch Society. (2015, August 17). '2030 Agenda': Latest UN plan for world government [online video]. Viewed September 18, 2015 at https://www.youtube.com/watch?v=zMj6BQ00BbM

Koltko-River, M., & Hancock, P.A. (2005). *The plausibility of the 'Bible Code' as a statistical artifact of differences between English and Hebrew*. Unpublished paper.

Koltko-Rivera, M. (2011). *Judgment Day? Not yet: Why the Rapture won't happen on May 21, 2011*. n.p.: Smashwords. Updated version, *Why Judgment Day didn't come: Why Harold Camping's predictions failed*, available online at http://www.smashwords.com/books/view/61086

List of 15th-century lunar eclipses [online encyclopedia article]. (2015). Retrieved September 17, 2015 from https://en.wikipedia.org/wiki/List_of_15th-century_lunar_eclipses

List of 20th-century lunar eclipses [online encyclopedia article]. (2015). Retrieved September 17, 2015 from https://en.wikipedia.org/wiki/List_of_20th-century_lunar_eclipses

List of 21st-century lunar eclipses [online encyclopedia article]. (2015). Retrieved September 16, 2015 from https://en.wikipedia.org/wiki/List_of_21st-century_lunar_eclipses

Melanson, T. (2009). *Perfectibilists: The 18th century Bavarian Order of the Illuminati.* Walterville, OR: Trine Day LLC.

Online Data Robert Schiller [web page]. (n.d.). Consulted September 14, 2015 at http://www.econ.yale.edu/~shiller/data.htm

Order of the Solar Temple [online encyclopedia article]. Retrieved May 15, 2011 from http://en.wikipedia.org/wiki/Order_of_the_Solar_Temple

Perkins, B. (n.d.). Blood Moon madness [web page]. *Rapture Ready.* Retrieved September 17, 2015 from https://www.raptureready.com/soap2/perkins12.html

Phillips, T. (2014). A tetrad of lunar eclipses [online news article]. Retrieved September 16, 2015 from http://science.nasa.gov/science-news/science-at-nasa/2014/27mar_tetrad/

Poole, S. M. (2011, May 14). Will Christ return May 21? *The Atlanta Journal-Constitution* [online edition]. Available at http://www.ajc.com/lifestyle/will-christ-return-may-945589.html

Pound, T. (2015, August 30). A look at market cycle theories: What works, what doesn't, and does it matter? [online article]. *Seeking Alpha* [website]. Retrieved September 14, 2015, from (registration required) http://seekingalpha.com/artiocle/3476776-a-look-at-market-cycle-theories-what-works-what-doesn't-and-does-it-matter

Price, L. (2015, January 31). The final Blood Moon: Sept, 2015 – prepare now [online video]. Viewed September 18, 2015, at https://www.youtube.com/watch?v=II0EWm2aXzo

Prothero, S. (2008). *Religious literacy: What every American needs to know—and doesn't*. New York, NY: HarperOne. (Original work published 2007)

Red Moon Rapture [website]. (2009). Viewed September 17, 2015 at https://redmoonrapture.com/

Reich, R. B. (2011). *Aftershock: The next economy and America's future*. New York, NY: Vintage/Random House.

Shire, E. (2015, September 17). Anti-Semites flock to Ann Coulter's side [online news article]. *The Daily Beast*. Retrieved September 18, 2015 from http://www.thedailybeast.com/articles/2015/09/17/why-ann-coulter-s-anti-semitism-is-dangerous.html

Shmita [online encyclopedia article]. Retrieved September 10, 2015 from https://en.wikipedia.org/wiki/Shmita

SignsofThyComing. (2014, November 18). Blood Moon : False prophet Pope Francis to visit the Beast during Super Blood Moon [online video]. Viewed September 13, 2015 at https://www.youtube.com/watch?t=1&v=M1E1nSOsjNU

Snyder, M. (2015, August 20). The big list of 33 things that are going to happen in September 2015 [online news article]. *Alex Jones' Infowars.com*. Retrieved September 13, 2015, from http://www.infowars.com/the-big-list-of-33-things-that-are-going-to-happen-in-september-2015/

Sokol, S. (2015, July 7). PLO ambassador endorses Protocols of the Elders of Zion [online news story]. *The Jerusalem Post* [online edition]. Retrieved September 18, 2015 from http://www.jpost.com/Arab-Israeli-Conflict/PLO-ambassador-endorses-Protocols-of-the-Elders-of-Zion-408250

Styxhexenhammer666. (2015, July 27). September prophecies: Shemitah, Blood Moons, Nibiru, Asteroid Etc [online video]. Viewed September 18, 2015 at https://www.youtube.com/watch?v=L_kYRlHjbvc

Taylor, M. (n.d.). Blood Moon rising – Day of the Lord [web page]. *Rapture Ready*. Retrieved September 17, 2015 from https://www.raptureready.com/soap/taylor83.html

Top scientists issue huge alert: Everything in place to open gates of Hell this year—2015 [online news article]. (2015, March 15). *Before It's News*. Retrieved September 17, 2015 from http://beforeitsnews.com/prophecy/2015/03/top-scientists-issue-huge-alert-everything-in-place-to-open-gates-of-hell-this-year-2015-and-we-should-be-very-concerned-this-is-absolutely-shocking-shocking-videos-must-see-2467904.html

Tversky, A., & Kahneman, D. (2004). Judgment under uncertainty: Heuristics and biases. In E. Shafir (Ed.), *Preference, belief, and similarity: Selected writings by Amos Tversky* (pp. 203-230). Cambridge, MA: The MIT Press. (Original work published in the 27 September 1974 issue of *Science, 185*, 1124-1131.)

United Nations. (2015). *Transforming our world: The 2030 Agenda for Sustainable Development* [draft document]. New York, NY: Author. Retrieved September 17, 2015 from http://www.un.org/ga/search/view_doc.asp?symbol=A/69/L.85&Lang=E

United Nations Sustainable Development Summit 2015 [web page]. (2015). Retrieved September 17, 2015 from https://sustainabledevelopment.un.org/post2015/summit

U.S. Religious Knowledge Survey (online document). (2010, Sept. 28). Available as of May 15, 2011 at http://pewforum.org/U-S-Religious-Knowledge-Survey-Who-Knows-What-About-Religion.aspx

Weiss, R., & Brackman, L. (2015, September 11). Poll: 70% of European Jews conceal their religion [online news article]. *Ynetnews/Jewish World*. Retrieved September 18, 2015 from http://www.ynetnews.com/articles/0,7340,L-4699567,00.html

About the Author

Mark Koltko-Rivera, Ph.D. holds a doctoral degree from the Department of Applied Psychology at New York University (NYU). He has presented is research under a variety of auspices, including the North Atlantic Treaty Organization (NATO) and the U.S. Army Science Conference. He is an elected Fellow of the American Psychological Association. For his scholarship, he has received several awards: the Margaret Gorman Early Career Award in the psychology of religion (from the Society for the Psychology of Religion and Spirituality), the Carmi Harari Early Career Award for Inquiry (Society for Humanistic Psychology), and, on two occasions, the George A. Miller Award for an outstanding recent article on general psychology (Society for General Psychology). He has taught (including statistics and research design) at NYU, the University of Central Florida, and elsewhere. His articles have appeared in *Review of General Psychology*, *Journal of Humanistic Psychology*, *Peace Psychology*, and elsewhere.

He graduated from Regis High School (NYC), and also holds an undergraduate degree from Haverford College, and a master's degree from Fordham University.

Mark is an active member of The Church of Jesus Christ of Latter-day Saints. He served for two years as an LDS missionary in the Japan Okayama Mission. He has published about the Latter-day Saints in *Sunstone, Dialogue: A Journal of Mormon Thought*, and *Psychotherapy*. He is the author of *The Rise of the Mormons: Latter-day Saint Growth in the 21st Century* (2012) and *Latter-day Saint Women and the Priesthood of God*.

He welcomes visits to his website: www.koltkorivera.com.